Social anxiety
Ultimate guide to overcome your shyness and fear

Mike Bray

Mike Bray

ISBN-13: 978-1542785075

ISBN-10: 1542785073:

Introduction:

Social anxiety is a disorder characterized by emotional discomfort, fear, apprehension, and worry about social situations that could potentially expose a person to public scrutiny and evaluation. It is also directly tied to the fear of social interaction.

In other words, this is a condition that is based on fear of receiving negative criticism from others, leading to feeling of inadequacy, embarrassment, humiliation and depression. These are often so intense that people who have social phobia often go through lengths to avoid situations that will force them to interact with other people or to do the things that they are fearful about. Its nickname, 'crippling shyness,' appropriately describes how debilitating this condition to those who experience it.

Difference Between Specific Social Anxiety And Generalized Social Anxiety

Specific social anxiety, as the name suggests, is focused on 1 or 2 things that can make a person particularly nervous. This could include fear of speaking in public, of doing something particular in public such as eating or drinking with other people, speaking with authority figures or going on a date. Generalized social anxiety, meanwhile, is anxiety over being uncomfortable, nervous or excessively anxious in almost all social situations.

What are the situations that people with this disorder fear and try to avoid.

People suffering from with either condition usually experience significant emotional distress when faced with two types of situations: performance situations (or situations that force them to perform in front of others or allow other people to observe them) and social interaction situations (or situations that force them to interact with people). Most people who are suffering from social anxiety try to avoid both types of situations.

Examples of performance situations that people with social anxiety fear and avoid are speaking in public, being introduced to people, being the center of attention, interpersonal relationships, public performances and addresses, being in public places, and doing something in public.

Examples of social interaction situations that people

dealing with this condition fear to be intimate with someone, talking to strangers, initiating and marinating conversation, going on a date or a party, being assertive, and expressing personal opinions.

Symptoms

When under such situations, a person dealing with social anxiety would suffer from a host of physiological and psychological symptoms such overwhelming fear, racing heart, drying of the mouth, muscle freezing, difficulty swallowing, extreme self-consciousness and heart palpitations.

Causes

There are two causes of Social anxiety- biological factors and psychological factors. Biological factors include abnormal brain activity in response to normal events and situations, abnormal levels of specific neurotransmitters in the brain, and genetic make-up of the person. On the other hand, psychological factors include previous experience of trauma regarding social situations, having better ability to pay attention to socially threatening people and events, having negative beliefs about social situations, and greater tendency to be anxious.

Do you think you overcame your shyness and fear? If you defeated social anxiety, you do not feel shy or afraid of talking to other people anymore, but you are not sure how to do it, check out as well book titled " Conversation: 7 communication techniques and tactics to win small talks" **to learn how to start, maintain and end conversation!**

Call for Review

Thank you very much for buying my book, hopefully you get the value you want to get. Please, if you found this book helpful, review it on amazon pages so that other people can see pros and cons of this book, and as well it is very good indicator for me as an author what to improve, avoid or keep. Thank you very much!

CONTENTS

Table of Contents

Social Anxiey

Chapter 1. Reasons for Shyness and Fear

Low Self-Confidence

The story

Jane faces an important decision: she has to choose a university and a major, which will determine her future career. Jane has been passionate about astronomy since she was a child. She wakes up every day and checks NASA's main page for updates and really wants to be a space scientist.

However, she wanted to ask her classmates first what they thought about it. She felt she needed confirmation. Her classmates told her it was interesting, however, when she left the conversation they started talking about how difficult it is to get into a university with a space science program. Only 5-10 percent of people who apply actually make it, and surely, Jane would not be among those people.

Jane overheard this conversation and processed it with mixed feelings – mixed negative feelings. On one hand, she agreed with her classmates, there was no way she would be in that top 5-10 percent so she decided to not even apply. On the other hand, she felt a deep self-resentment that she was stupid enough to tell such a hilarious idea to other human beings. However, her main conclusion was still this: no trying means no shame and no failure.

The problem

People who lack confidence in their own value and capabilities, and who lack trust in themselves or others can be easily influenced. Of course, this is truer when this influence is about convincing them of their own incompetence. When it comes to positive influence, it takes a lot of effort and energy to make them believe in their strengths. They rarely truly believe.

Here I would like to emphasize a distinction that must be made: low self-confidence and shyness are different characteristics. A person can be shy without lacking confidence and vice versa – a person can have low confidence and not be shy.

Shyness is more often a quality of introverted people. It is a learned behavior. Shyness is a form of reluctance to be naturally social and open. Low self-confidence, on the other hand, is always related to internal problems and feelings of inadequacy.

A feeling of inadequacy is triggered when a person thinks she has made a mistake in front of others. She also fears that these people will tell other people of her inadequacy so she begins to panic, then starts to berate and hate herself for her stupidity.

She can even fall into a vicious cycle of self-loathing where she not only reacts to the triggering incident, but she also starts dreading the possibility of making other mistakes. More often than not, she does attract another unpleasant experience. She loses her temper with her loved ones because her tensions run high, then she

forgets something, **etc.** Trying to avoid looking foolish at feared events, she may isolate herself from new discussions or stay quiet in order to make sure she doesn't say anything wrong. Or, she stops initiating conversations and even (as we saw in the story of Jane) stops working for better opportunities because she feels inadequate.

The benefits of high self-confidence

The overall benefits of self-confidence can be summarized with these keywords: higher self-worth, less stress, less anxiety or fear, freedom from self-doubt, more happiness and enjoyment, better social interactions, better sleep, and so on.

Generally, you'll feel better about yourself by being yourself. This doesn't mean you'll never come to a crossroads where you get caught up in momentary self-doubt or hesitate to make a decision, but you accept this short, negative resonance as a natural part of being human. You become comfortable with it, and confident that even if you hit a low note from time to time, higher notes that will come along soon.

People with high self-confidence make a lot of mistakes just like anyone else, but, unlike others, they don't let these mistakes take over their attitude. Mistakes and failures become the main source of feedback that helps them readjust their actions.

The solution

The best way to overcome the lack of self-confidence and gradually become ok with ourselves is to think about WHY we feel the way we do about ourselves.

If we feel that we can't accomplish something we have to find the inner strength to analyze this situation logically. If the discouragement comes from within, we have to seek the answers from within as well. For example, you can always ask the following three questions of yourself when you hit a low point:

1. *Why do I feel like this about myself? Why do I think I'm not good enough?*

2. Is the scenario I'm afraid of a realistic one? Even if it happens, what's the worst consequence?

3. *Do I want to change my feelings toward this problem? Yes? What can I do now to take the first step?*

Very few people actually stop and think about why they feel certain bad feelings and uncertainties. They'd rather get rid of them by complaining about them. The more people they complain to the less they feel it (so they might think). But, in reality, this is not a solution, but oftentimes it is a cause. People trap themselves in negative cycles by constantly complaining.

If you want more confidence, you have to stop considering yourself a victim. Consider yourself a survivor who can go as far as possible. If you slowly but surely cut out complaining from your life, you'll be much more positive and sanguine.

Low self-confidence is not only triggered by internal stimuli but also external. There are many people out there with different stories, opinions, and tragedies. You cannot always prevent bumping into them or avoid interactions with them, but you can decide what you actually believe and take from these interactions.

Always consider the source first. Don't buy relationship advice from someone who struggles with it. Don't hire a fat personal trainer if you want to lose weight. Don't choose a financial advisor who is poor and has never been rich. I could share many more examples like this.

Don't take what others say for granted. How do you do this? Ask the following three questions when somebody judges you:

1. *Do I look up to this person in the area he/she is talking about?*
2. Does he live by his own advice?

3. If she is a good model for positive affirmations, can they be applied to my life too?

If you answer YES to all three questions, then it's almost certain you can trust this person in what they say and you can consider buying the advice they are selling.

If, however, you answered any of these questions with no, then think twice or maybe three times about how much credit you should give and how personal should you should take anything you just heard. Remember Jane's story and the opportunity she missed because she listened to what some eighteen-year-old yahoos told her.

Never stop doing your own thing. Individuals with high confidence are how they are, and they do what they do, because they love doing it. They don't slow down, change, or stop for anyone who deems their actions inappropriate.

Catastrophizing

The Story

Chloe wakes up with a bright smile on her lips. She feels happy, but when she turns over in her bed she notices that her boyfriend left without saying a word. Her stomach freezes and a cold chill runs up her spine. You know, that typical bad feeling you have when something unexpectedly hurts your soul.

She jumps out of bed and starts looking for a note. No note. She desperately tries to recall what she may have said or done the night before that made him angry. For a moment, she thought maybe she was sleep-talking about the hot barista she chats with when she grabs a coffee. But it's not like that, she doesn't like him like that. What if her boyfriend wants to break up now? What if he already found somebody, this very morning! Serendipity, it's Christmas!

And all this is based on what? Her assumptions and lack of emotional confidence.

I can see you now thinking about whether this is so like you, or thinking quite the opposite – what a BS, who does that? Well, more people than you think.

The problem

Many people that you'd never expect catastrophize. This person seems normal and confident during their day, and collected at work. But sometimes, minor events can kick them off-balance into a pit of worst worst-case scenarios.

Why do I say this? Because people who are genuinely aware of their lack of confidence live in a constant state of worst-case scenarios. For them, expecting the worst is not shocking, it's normal.

Catastrophizing people, on the other hand, think they are confident, but, in fact, they are not. Their main issue is that they are unaware of or deny their own lack of confidence. In order to move on and reduce the catastrophizing tendency, the first step is to realize and/or accept that they are vulnerable and sometimes insecure.

The greatest danger with catastrophism is that people consider themselves ok, and their catastrophe is shocking. As a result, they take it much more seriously and determinatively. They will start to fear their present, positive state is **temporary**, and something will **always** come that will ruin it. They will start expecting it day by day – today, today sh@t will happen. And without further ado, they transform themselves into a genuinely insecure person who always expects the worst.

The benefits of a catastrophe-free life

"I've had a lot of worries in my life, most of which never happened," Mark Twain said once. And this is very true. Life has many ups and downs anyway, why create problems where there aren't any?

Living a bit outside of our head can be helpful sometimes. I tell this to people who occasionally or always expect negative outcomes. There is no magical one-sentence formula for how to stop catastrophe creation; you simply have to commit to stop doing it.

The solution

The first step is to recognize catastrophizing. Then commit to challenge it as many times as is necessary to stop it.

Find the patterns: what triggers this response in you? I'd say it's usually an insignificant emotional, or mental experience. Therefore, the negative thought association is blown out of proportion until you reach the absolute worst-case scenario.

1. Cut the cycle!

Be there mentally when it happens. You are the only one who can control what happens inside your brain. Stop it. You can even tell yourself **STOP STOP STOP**, to distract your mind. Start singing your favorite song or start reading aloud from a book. Focus on each letter as you read -- punctuation, anything. Flip yourself out of the spiral.

2. When you can see out of the spiral ask yourself: is this real?

Why do I think this? What did that other person do wrong? What did I do wrong? In most cases, just asking and answering these questions makes you realize that all that happened in your head only happened there. There is no chance for it to happen in the real world.

3. If point 2 is not enough

If, however, following point 2 does not help, there is another solution, the other side of the coin: jump right to the bottom. Do not spend an hour putting together a thought thread to reach the worst-case scenario, but jump straight there to Dante's ninth hell from the start, bang!

When you phrase your greatest fear, you can instantly switch to a positive spiral to think about how you can prevent this bad scenario. Then, as you would have spiraled downwards, now spiral upwards with your thoughts, and figure out a systematic solution for how to prevent or avoid that bad outcome. When you reach the top of your spiral, most of the time you will realize that if you just do not disturb the status quo, nothing bad will happen.

If you feel that there is some reality in your bad expectation, then do your best to avoid it. It is never too late.

Arrogance and Aggression

The story

The following story will go through the jealous reaction of a wife who found a phone number written on a napkin in her husband's pocket. The first monologue will present what she said. The second will be what she thought.

- "What's this paper? I just found it in your pocket! Whose number is this? Are you cheating on me? Did you talk to another woman? I know you did! You are just like your father! Why do you do this to me? What did I do to deserve this?"

The text above expresses lots of insecurities and different emotional abuse techniques. First, there is an aggressive penetration of the other's private sphere. The wife holds her husband accountable for the paper she just found in an unauthorized search. In the next step, she expresses a clear lack of trust: "Are you cheating?" She does not even consider other options. Maybe the note is from a male acquaintance. Maybe it is from a business opportunity. She goes right to cheating. The third attack is a negative, belittling comparison: "you're just like your father." She attacks her husband with something that is a fact; his father is a womanizer, but not direct proof of his dishonesty. In addition, to put the cherry on the whipped cream, she makes herself the victim.

Let us see what she is thinking:

- "I found this paper... what can that be? He will not tell me unless I am firm enough. He might lie. He cheats. I am sure he would. However, why wouldn't he? I am older now, after the kids, my skin is not as elastic as it was. I am so tired; we do not often have sex. I do not even desire him. I do not like myself. Who would like me? Who would find me attractive? Still, this is no reason for dishonesty! I will tell him! He'll see who he is messing with!"

Many insecurities and things she does not usually talk about - surface in her inner monologue. She is aware she is part of the problem, but when it comes to expressing it to her husband, she does not admit it. She does not admit that she knows she is less attractive, that their love life is deteriorating, and that while cheating is nasty, it is not so surprising. She plays the victim instead.

Even though she knows she is not perfect either, she does not admit it or truly accept it. If she did, she could have a more open and real conversation about the problems they face as a couple. If the husband indeed cheated, it means they should have talked about their issues much earlier. However, it is always better to have the conversation later than not at all.

Even though the wife seems aggressive and arrogant on the outside, she faces some serious self-hatred and is unfulfilled on the inside. She is too proud and scared to talk about her feelings so she keeps her tough, **do not mess with me** face on. Thus, she will not be able to solve the problem, but at least she will win the argument.

The problem

The story of this chapter has two major issues. The first is an aggressive manifestation of worst-case scenario creation. However, the bigger problem is a deep insecurity that comes from self-loathing, aggression, and emotional abuse.

Leaving our story aside, insecurity of this level can lead to the development of social withdrawal or even paranoia. This may turn into compensatory behaviors such as aggression or bullying. Insecurity is distressing and has a threatening impact on people's psyches. Some might become the silent killer types of people who are reserved and silent, but deal with their fears inside themselves. However, insecurity can also turn a person into a controlling personality, which is also a defensive psychological reaction.

Fear and anxiety are the cornerstones of emotional insecurity. Most of the time they are rooted in early life experiences, when people create their perspectives on how they fit in the world. If they get mostly negative feedback and a withdrawal of love as punishment from their parents, they will not feel adequate, lovable, worthy, or good enough later on. Having such a start in life, they grow into fearful and anxious adults, always on guard, disappointed, and expecting the worst.

If insecurity takes an extreme form, it affects everything in a person's life. In addition, when I say everything, I mean it. It twists the person's ability to make sensible decisions, to maintain ambition, to handle disappointments. They lose basic emotional stability, energy, the ability to objectively analyzing and learn from their mistakes, openness to new things, improving skills, and the ability to be introspective.

The benefit of overcoming possessive behavior

I can summarize it in a few, but meaningful words: peace of mind, healthy relationships, less mental clutter and a life beyond fears.

The solution

a.) If your partner has aggressive or possessive behavior

If you are the victim of a possessive person, first assume

the best – they may not be aware they are acting possessively. Start by telling them how their behavior makes you feel. For example:

"When you check what I was doing when you're not with me, it makes me feel like you don't trust me. I don't think this is fair."

Do not give them names; for example, do not call possessive or harassing people maniacs. When you describe your problems do not direct them at them, but at their behavior. For example:

"You acted possessively" instead of "You're a possessive person."

If you give them a bad name, they might argue with you, but if you call out the emotion, it triggered in you, they cannot argue.

If that is not enough, you can talk with him calmly about the behaviors you are not willing to tolerate. Bring up only the things that you are not willing to compromise on. Be specific.

"I do not accept that you search my phone and belongings."
"I do not like it when you make me feel guilty and, as a result, I have to change my plans."

Since possessive behavior is a sign of low self-confidence and inadequacy, make sure to assure your partner that you are determined to be by his or her side. It can be a bit tiring sometimes, especially if your partner needs constant assurance. However, if you want the relationship to work smoothly, **step out of your assurance comfort zone and tell them more times for your partner's sake**. However, give your partner a deadline for when they must come around and trust you without reassuring words. For example, if your partner needs this kind of assurance on a weekly basis even after five years, then it is not ok.

If you feel that the relationship has become toxic because of the repeated obsessive and possessive behavior, it is time to consider leaving the relationship. If you spent time trying to make things better, if you even tried counseling, but nothing brought results, it's time to put your own interests and wellbeing before anything else.

Be prepared, the break up will not be easy or without attempts at emotional abuse. However, do not let yourself be blackmailed. Possessive people become sure, usually after a good amount of time, that if there is something wrong in the relationship, it is because of you, not them. In addition, they will not hesitate to express this when they feel they are in danger. Just like the wife in the example, the partner might try to be aggressive (hopefully **only** with words), and making unfair comparisons. Alternatively, they will simply step into the victim's shoes and try to make you feel sorry for them. In addition, many times, this works.

I am sure you have some friends who have been in toxic relationships for years because their partner "wouldn't survive" without them. You, being an outsider, can see clearly what is going on and how manipulated your friend is. However, being objective in your own case, well that is a different story because you are so emotionally involved.

In extreme cases, a possessive partner might even try to threaten suicide or use another highly abusive tool just to make you stay. It is very difficult to stick with your decision if this much fear is triggered. If things escalate to this level, you might want to consider involving a professional, an attorney, or at least your friends and family in the breakup.

If you are married or in a long-term relationship, and you have decided to separate from your partner, do not do it on impulse. Prepare everything in advance: speak with your attorney about the details of the divorce, prepare mentally with your counselor, and tell your most trusted friends about it for moral support. Also, anticipate a harsh reaction from your partner. By now, you know your partner better than anyone. If you think there is a chance that your partner's reaction will threaten your safety, it is better to leave and let the person know about your decision by phone.

If children are involved, try to make the separation as smooth for them as possible. Tell your partner that your decision is final, but for the sake of the children, you need to stay under the same roof in a calm environment until the divorce or separation process is through. You can specify that if your partner needs to discuss the separation you are only willing to have it in the counselor's office.

Even if you know that the relationship ended because of your partner's possessive behavior, it does not mean you will not be affected emotionally. Healing takes time even if you feel relieved. You can always get professional help; there is no shame in it. Give yourself time to get over all the shocks and bad feelings you gathered over the years. Getting physical distance from an abusive partner is just the first step.

b.) If you are the one exhibiting aggressive and possessive behavior.

First things first – it is already a great achievement for you to acknowledge that you have been acting the wrong way. You would not believe how rare it is that somebody is self-aware enough to recognize and admit to bad behavior.

Now that you know it, we can agree that you have to change certain things in the future to make your own life, and the lives of those you love.

We are not born with aggressive and possessive behavior. These are learned patterns and they root somewhere in your childhood and early adulthood. How do we clean our garden efficiently? If we pull out all the weeds by their roots. Therefore, your first task is to clean up your garden, and to find the roots of all the weeds that suffocate the beautiful flowers.

Do you act possessively? Why? What is the reason you feel the need to act this way? What are you afraid of? Why do you think you are not enough for your partner?

These are difficult questions to ask yourself. You may feel a lot of pain. However, pain is good, it cleanses you. There is no major change without pain. Yes, you have to deal with remorse of all the bad or hurtful things you have done.

However, that is over now. You know what the problems are, and you are willing to change them. You are a good person, a caring person; there is nothing wrong with you that deprives you from being loved. That is why your partner sticks with you in the first place. They believe in you! So, believe in yourself and start making changes, which will benefit everyone, especially you. It will not be a short process, so be patient, give yourself time.

You have to leave the past behind you. Maybe you were fooled, cheated on, and everything feels terrible, but note that your current partner is not the one who caused you pain. If one man or woman cheated, it does not mean all of them will. So, if the person with you did not hurt you, why would you hurt them? Do not let the previous bad experience ruin your present chance for happiness.

Living in the past is like stomping all over your plants in an effort to kill the poisonous scorpion that attacked you when it is already far, far away. You do not kill the scorpion, but you do manage to kill everything good around you.

Do not be violent. The more you pressure your partner with your doubt and possessiveness, the further you will push them away. Nobody wants to be with a person who is constantly scared and suffocates him or her with all his or her accumulated fear and worry about love. Your partner loves you. That is why they decided to be with you. So, if you get freedom, give freedom. Let them have fun without you, and do not screw them when they come home. If your partner has not done anything wrong and you start blaming them anyway, they might start wondering whether it is worth it to be good and faithful when the results are the same.

Live your own life let them live theirs, and when you are together share the best of both. Have your own work, hobbies, and social life. Do not spend all your time with your partner just to be able to keep an eye on them. If you do things separately that you can share afterwards, you will always be an interesting person. It is important to spend time together, but it is also fun if you spend time apart from each other and do different things you can share and talk about when you are together.

Get to know your partner's friends, and let them know yours. It is a great way to stop being jealous. If you know whom your partner spends time with, you will know that there is no cause for alarm.

Do not be ashamed to talk about your issues with possessiveness. When you know where they come from, tell your partner why they occur - past relationships, childhood traumas, **etc.** Do not assume that by telling your partner that you have good reasons to act as you do, that you are entitled to go on acting this way and that they must be considerate about it. However, you may gain some time and benevolence from your partner that may help you get over these things. Pay attention to the bad behavior patterns and get beyond them. If you need, contact a professional counselor to help you as an individual, or you as a couple.

Lethargy

The Story

Josh got an invitation from his friend, Brad, to celebrate his baby's first birthday with his family and close friends. Although he was very pleased by his friend's thoughtfulness, Josh felt a growing anxiety. He was never very outgoing or socially secure, but one year ago, when Brad's kid was born, they got together as a small group of friends to celebrate. That time he drank a bit more than usual and tried to pick up Brad's sister, Jessica, who publicly rejected him.

Since then, Josh has not gone out with his friends. He's spoken with Brad very little, and has been, in fact, convincing himself that he only doesn't want to bother Brad because of the baby. Josh lived the past months in a state of deep lethargy and isolation because whenever he bumped into one on his friends, he felt he was in the spotlight of ridicule. He was convinced everybody was still talking about his shame from the baby shower. What was he thinking? Jessica? Really? She is so out of his league.

Josh did not want to face the same people, especially Jessica, again because he would be rejected again, laughed at, and he would be the center of attention – not the baby. In addition, what if someone brought up last year is rejection? Ugh, he would be so humiliated. So why take the risk?

The problem

Emotionally insecure people become lethargic easily and often. Triggered by the fear of rejection, they can end up in an unhealthy lonely state. The adversity or stressor that causes lethargy can come from family issues, relationship problems, a poor health condition, or career and livelihood worries. Sometimes even childhood traumas can be responsible. A lethargic state can continue for years, or it can be temporary, and only appear when a similar, threatening situation appears.

It is not unusual for those who have experienced lethargy to have been abused or abandoned, and to be unable to realize they are in a lethargic state.

If you've suffered from many emotionally hurtful situations, you may feel the need to shield yourself from such experiences. In self-chosen isolation, it is easier to deny or avoid your feelings. Having been rejected repeatedly, whether verbally, emotionally, or physically, you may have also lowered your expectations of people and/or life in general. To give such a response to an adverse situation is not uncommon or irrational.

However, do not forget that not everybody is the same. If someone treated you badly or rejected you, it does not mean that you will always be rejected. Think about what you did wrong in the situation when you were rejected (if there was anything). In the story above, for example, Josh was a bit drunk when he approached Jessica. Maybe if he followed a more traditional way of courting, he would have been successful. He meant no harm, and he was publicly rejected. Since public opinion matters to him a great deal, this event affected him a lot. The solution to his problem would be to simply apologize to Jessica for his bad behavior (especially if the topic comes up) and move on. He would feel redeemed, and everybody would probably think positively of him for his strength of character.

The benefit of overcoming lethargy

Do not forget that at the end of the day happiness is a decision. The emotionally strong understand the great power their brains have over their mind and body. They know that emotions are reactions to their thoughts, and how they perceive a certain event.

In other words, your emotions do not reflect reality, but the way you choose to interpret reality. If you accept this, you will be able to get almost total control over your emotions.

This means that there is no bad event, rejection, or catastrophe that can make you feel sad and under the weather without your consent. In addition, the amazing thing is that when you let it go, it goes. The moment you decide that this event is not changing who you are, you realize that indeed it is true. In addition, who are these other people to judge you? Show me someone with a perfect life who has never made a mistake or had a weird derailment. If someone still wants to judge you, that person is a hypocrite and you should not make a moment of your life miserable working for his or her approval.

The solution

Emotionally strong people do not expose themselves to people who crush their morale. Many people around you are lost and, willingly or unwillingly, can take you along with them. Do not let an awful acquaintance or a bad event ruin your happiness. Lethargy is not always something that people create for themselves. Staying in a lethargic environment is quite contagious.

When you start feeling lethargic without reason, take the time to objectively examine the attitude of the people you spend most of your time with. There is a saying that your attitude is a mishmash of the attitudes of five people with whom you are most connected to. If some or all of these five people are lethargic, negative, complaining, defeatist, there you go – reason detected. Slowly try to make new friends, surround yourself with people whose attitudes are similar to what you would like to have.

If you feel afraid to open up to other people or fall in love, it could mean that you still carry some unhealed scars and do not have enough confidence in yourself. You do not need to be perfectly healed or very confident to initiate a relationship. Nobody in this world is without scars and always in peak confidence. To be honest, it would be quite intimidating to meet someone like that.

If you fear, initiating any relationship because you think you will surely mess something up. Thus, any relationship would be doomed from the beginning and you choose to stay alone, in lethargy, because you do not want to get hurt again – that is not ok. Your days are precious, and they will never come back.

Decide to be brave. Get out of the state of lethargy. Ask yourself if it is better to stay sorrowful and alone, or take a risk and find something better. You are a social being and you will feel much better if you find positive people who are likeminded and who you can connect with and establish a judgment-free relationship together. These people are somewhere outside and waiting to be found. You will never find them if you do not try.

Of course, select the people you choose to trust. As I said, many are lost and can easily hurt you or bring you down. Look for patterns in behavior, word usage, and body language to deduce what kind of person you are dealing with. If you do not like to be in that person's company, you owe him or her nothing. You can leave anytime.

Regarding past events when you felt embarrassed, take a deep breath and move on. It is history; you cannot change it. The more you mourn it, the worse you will feel. So, let it go. It does not matter anymore. Learn the lessons, do not react or act the same way again if it was inappropriate. If you need to, apologize. First, forgive yourself.

Practicing gratitude can also help you overcome

negative, self-limiting feelings. Tony Robbins says that if you have gratitude in your life, you will have no room for anger, ungratefulness, or fear. Try to collect every aspect of your life so you can practice this feeling of gratitude: collect at least five things you can be grateful for in this moment. They can be very basic physiological things like being healthy, being able to breathe, and more materialistic stuff such as owning a cool watch or having a huge TV.

Lethargy often comes together with physical tiredness and lack of motivation. You have to overcome this state not only mentally, but also physically. Boost your mood with 10-20 minutes of crazy dancing in your room without anyone watching. Put on your favorite jam from the '80s, let that Rolling Stones or Spice Girls sound into your ears. It is even funnier if you listen to music through your headphones. Imagine a crowd of people around you who are unable to hear what you are listening to, but they just see what you do. Imagine their puzzled, scandalized faces and laugh about them. Who cares? The jokes on them, you are having so much fun! Who is weirder: the one who lives through amazing moments, or the one who is consumed by bitterness? You decide.

Lastly, sometimes, feeling lethargic can be a sign of illness or depression. If you are continually feeling like it is hard to get going, but there is no specific event you can blame for your feeling of sadness (if even the people you surround yourself with are not at fault), I would suggest making an appointment to see your doctor. If you truly believe you did not let any external event affect you, it might be something internal. Just to make sure, check with a specialist.

Vulnerability

The Story

Let us pretend you play truth or dare with your friends. You are nervous and self-conscious about choosing dare, as many of us are, because you do not want to do anything compromising or embarrassing. Therefore, you pick truth.

The person in charge, asking the question is in an emotional mood, so he asks you what you dislike about yourself the most. There are four people in the game, and you know three of them. However, there is also a (nice) stranger girl. You start feeling uncomfortable. You really do not like to talk about your weaknesses in front of others. You like to maintain an image of yourself as somebody who is ok with himself, and who doesn't have anything he dislikes about himself.

Except the nose, the belly, the weird ass-shaped chin, his finger nails, his pimples, hisimpatience and deep insecurity, his intense wish to belong and feel loved, his deep scars from previous relationships that still affect his present relationships… Oh, no, you cannot tell them all these things. What will happen to your image? What will happen if you attract even more attention to your nose or, even worse, what if they notice you actually care?

Is talking about your insecurities a weakness? Will you be considered weaker if you admit how much mess are you dealing with internally? Will you be judged or become a laughing stock? Will people lose faith in your secure and seemingly well-composed character?

However, you have to tell the truth... This game is about truth, and you would feel ashamed if you lied. Therefore, you open your mouth, and with a shaky voice, awkwardly trying to find the right words, you pour everything out – the discontentment you feel toward yourself, the insecurities you carry, and everything that passed through your worried mind. It is out there, you are exposed and very, utterly vulnerable.

Actually, I did not name any character in this story, because this happened to me a few weeks ago. I am the boy, and I was playing this game with three other people. They are my only friends in San Francisco. They are not total strangers, but since I have been here for only for 2 months, I cannot say I know them well.

I am a confidence coach, and I write about self-development, as you read at the beginning of my book, on my website, or social media account. Does this mean I am untouched by negativity? Surely not. Not at all. I am getting better at overcoming my own fears and at sharing the paths, I have found to success with other people. I have had to become better at dealing with my own negative feelings.

However, the truth is, you cannot eliminate them forever. There is no magic solution that can eliminate fear, defeatism, or anxiety from the face of the Earth. However, there are antidotes, like awareness and acceptance, and when you see a negative pattern starting; you can choose to fight it. I chose to fight the fear I felt when I was asked this question.

What will these successful American people think of me if they know? Then I asked myself this question: **what will I think about myself if I do not take their curiosity seriously and I do not answer them honestly?**

Therefore, I gave them my honest answer. You know what happened. I felt better. I felt proud for not preaching nonsense to my readers, I overcame my fear, and I chose to be brave.

In addition, you know what else happened. It turned out that one of the boysfelt uncomfortable with her nose too. One of the people makes similar mistakes as I do when it comes to relationships. In addition, the game turned into an honest exchange of opinions and experiences. I did not feel alone with my problems, and I gave comfort to my friends, too. After this big realization, we started talking about how we are all coping with negativity, and how we can give each other good tips. I still feel empowered by that evening.

In addition, to push my vulnerability to the next level – I just put that experience in this book. Now you have read it, and know it. In addition, you can relate to me, or someone who is dealing with negative stuff herself can piss you that you just bought a book. I accept any opinion or judgment you have. This is the wonderful thing about embracing vulnerability: once you do it, you actually get rid of fear.

The problem

When we try to make others believe that we are not vulnerable, we lie. Everybody has that spot. However, that lie automatically generates fear in us: what if they figure it out? What if they judge my vulnerability and dishonesty?

So, you cause yourself additional fear. I am sure you lied to your parents about something when you were a kid, and then you were terrified about them discovering your lie. Alternatively, you lie to your partner about something, which is not exactly a white lie, or to your boss, or anybody… As soon as the lie leaves your mouth, you feel pressure – sometimes vividly and sometimes passively.

In addition, if you accumulate many lies, there is a greater chance that you will forget about some of them, and one idle day, you will accidentally reveal your own lie. In addition, that is much worse than being honest about a weakness. I have become very abstract so let me give you some examples of vulnerabilities you can lie about.

- When you apply for a job, you lie to your boss and say that you can handle stress very well. They hire you, but at the first busy closing period, you become irritated. Your

system collapses, like Windows does when the entire screen goes blue, and nobody has any idea what should be done. Impossible to turn off, impossible to restart – brain dead. If there is an IT specialist, or, in your case, a stress-handling mastermind, everything will be fine. However, do not forget, you were hired to be the stress-handling mastermind.

If you were to honestly admit that you are not good at dealing with pressure, you might not have gotten that job. However, in the end it will be a win-win: the company finds somebody better for that position, and you are not trapped in work you will very soon hate.

- The first date syndrome – where everybody is so cool, so funny, and so good. Relationship, no, I do not want to trap you, just fun, fun, and fun. Kids, I hate kids, I do not want kids from you. Do not worry; I am not a needy type. How often do we lie to women to make them believe we are the man they want us to be (based on our manly judgment)? Alternatively, women, how often do you tell us men that you want emotions, that you love to spend time with your partner, and that you are very good at working out problems to make us believe we just met Queen of our lives?

I am sure all of us have experienced both sides of the conversation – when you were telling more (or less) about who you really were, and then your date did. In addition, in a few weeks or months, the surprises start to come. The woman starts insisting on a relationship where they live in a bubble. The person starts forgetting the mushy words. Then you just sit, stare, and wonder who that other person really is.

I am not saying you should not try your best on a first date, but do not hide or lie about your core values because you think the other person would not approve. Isn't it much better to just be who you are? If you are a good match you will be accepted anyway, and if not, isn't it better to know that now?

These are typical patterns when we want to appear less vulnerable. We want short-term happiness, so we lie.

The benefits of vulnerability

Peace of mind comes as soon as you realize how important it is to embrace it. Embrace who you are. You can always fine-tune those qualities you do not feel good about, but you can only do it well if you first decide to love yourself as you are in that imperfect, vulnerable, and exposed state.

If you always say, you will love yourself when you are the person you want to be, that day will never come. The correct chronology is acceptance, love, and then change. Not the other way around.

What is the benefit of embracing vulnerability? An honest life. Where you do not have to fear judgment, or that you will be discovered because everything is out there. In addition, it is hard to believe, but trust me when I say; it will be your shield.

Being totally out there, accepting your goofy, mushy, meticulous, impatient, clumsy self is the greatest power you have. In this state, you will be the closest you can be to unbreakable. Know that yes, you are already broken; there is nothing to break anymore. You are a wonderful mosaic – a unique, colorful picture of your personality and emotional world.

The solution

This entire chapter was the fact, the problem, and the solution in one. I really did not divide the flow of into the shape you have become accustomed to in the previous chapters because vulnerability is not really an emotional problem. It is emotional power if you are willing to use it. True, it can also be a weakness. However, it is only a weakness if you try to hide or deny it.

If you dare to open up, being vulnerable means that you are willing to open up to new experiences. Without vulnerability, it is hard to develop your ability to connect with others and to fully experience and accept yourself. People connect best through their vulnerabilities. I can tell, I have experienced it myself.

Vulnerability indeed means being open to experiences, giving fear your middle finger and accepting that things may not work out as you had hoped. Without it, as I said before, it is hard to be open to new things that are uncertain such as love, trust, friendship, and creativity.

Needing Attention

The story

Nina is constantly in the need of external feedback. She only considers a day well spent if at least two people complimented her.

However, she is not an unlikable character, who wishes recognition based on nothing, she works hard for it. Too hard, actually.

She always compliments her superiors on their great work, even if it is just a sketch of the actual project to come. She bakes for her colleagues every Monday and Friday, wishing them a good week and a good weekend. She also speaks very often and very loudly about her accomplishments.

Overall, she does not seem like a bad person. In addition, she bakes very well. However, is Nina truly happy and satisfied? No. She is exhausted every day. She never feels like the compliments are enough; she knows something is missing. Even if people like her, she needs more attention all the time.

However, why does she need so much feedback, so much reassurance? Because her own opinion of herself is not a good, and when others tell her otherwise she feels temporarily happy.

The problem

Needing attention is connected to the need to be loved. People like Nina who feel they need appreciative words only feel valuable and important when others make them feel needed. They are people pleasers, but for the wrong reasons. They do not want promotions or financial benefit as much as words about their worthiness.

The issue with this kind of behavior is that they will never feel truly happy or satisfied. Instead of chasing their own wishes, they chase the wishes of others, thus they never feel fulfilled. Not to mention it is super exhausting to try to please more than one person – that one person should be yourself.

The benefit of pleasing yourself first

People who have a great deal of self-worth do not do things they do not want to do. There are things that they do not love to do, but they do them anyway, otherwise the dirty dishes run away after a while. However, they have the self-respect to not do stuff that would conflict with their values.

Emotional strength allows you to focus on being able to do what you love instead of constantly avoiding what you hate. Thus, you get more knowledge about what you need to do, in order to do what you love.

Feeling genuine happiness will not only make your life

better, but it will also improve the lives of those around you. If you are ok with yourself, it will be visible to others and people will appreciate it. They will want to be like you. I have never heard of anybody who wanted to bake cookies on Thursday because Nina inspired them. However, if they saw Nina being happy and balanced – going to yoga and squash, eating donuts, and wearing red lipstick even though beauty magazines say it is out of style – they would love to have her life. Therefore, they would go, congratulate her, and ask in an awkward, dopey voice, "um, what's your secret?" In addition, Nina would get her attention.

The solution

Attention: cliché coming – find out who you are. But really, if you don't know yet, then summarize yourself in a nutshell here, and think about what would please you the most. Not others, you. If you already know, then accept it. Do not be afraid of it or what others may think of it that is probably the greatest thing you will ever do.

Here are some ideas for self-pleasing possibilities:

1. Choose to get lost in a creative art.

If you are living for the happiness of others, it is not difficult to be inauthentic to yourself. This is, in fact, the purpose of your actions, to be more like what others want you to be. However, doing something creative is a great way to express yourself in an authentic manner. It is an easy and enjoyable way to practice being you. You can choose painting, music, singing, constructing, or writing.

2. Beyond art, figure out methods and exercises for how to practice being more authentic to yourself.

Repeat these every day. Do not think about too complicated of stuff, it can mean doing something you enjoy by yourself, like reading, watching anime, or knitting. You can also write a list of positive affirmations about yourself that you recite every morning.

Practice being who you are and act in a way that feels genuine – ha-ha, what a bold thing to say, right? However, seriously, forget about worrying what others might say. You cannot influence that, and it is not your business. It is proof of their lack of character if they spend their precious time mocking you. Aren't they the ones who should be pitied if that is the highlight of their day?

The other good thing about authenticity is that you can practice being who you are anywhere anytime – only your presence is needed, and luckily that is something you have 24/7. Be spontaneous. For example, when you are in front of a vegan place, but you'd like to eat a steak, just admit it and say, "Actually, I don't like to eat vegan food that much even though my two best friends are vegan." Then grab your steak, you carnivore!

Be authentic with what you wear. If you prefer sporty clothes that are comfortable instead of high-fashion ones, just put them on. If you must dress up for work you can still wear a mishmash of comfy and elegant clothes – today there are so many less sporty, more casual, designer sportswear lines that it's almost impossible not to find something that satisfies you and your workplace's demands.

3.   Use social media wisely.

Social media platforms can often be misused by attention-seeking folks. People tend to give too much credit to what is happening or not happening in their virtual lives. I am always debating whether I find social media to be a lifesaver or a life ruiner.

As long as you use these web interfaces to make plans with friends and keep in touch with the people who live far away from you, it is a lifesaver. However, if you notice that you are using them only to share the highlights of your life to make others jealous, interested, or pissed, you should think about not posting.

What are the most common signs that you only seek attention on social media?

- If most of your posts have a bragging tone, or are about showing off and self-congratulation. Alternatively, the worst kind: "I'm bored. Like my post and I'll tell you…"

- If your posts express that you are feeling sorry for yourself, or that you are seeking compliments and support. Like if you say, "People always leave me. Why do I have to find only the dishonest ones?" I agree, it sucks to be disappointed or let down, but not everybody has to know about it. Talk about your problems with your closest friends and family only. Your Facebook "friends" mostly do not care or your misery may come as welcome news – at least not only their lives suck.

- Another kind of attention-seeking post could be, "I'm having so much fun at this awesome party with these awesome people!" Come on everybody, be jealous! Is the unwritten thought that follows? I am not saying you should not share happy moments from your life. It is better if you share happy thoughts than sad ones, but maybe you can phrase your post differently. Instead of the title above you can say something like, "So blessed to have so many great people around me."

Overconfidence

The story

Don Little is the deputy director of a small company. His specialty lies in doing little (as his name suggests) and saying much. He acts like a boss and corrects his employees all the time. He knows the best jokes, has the craziest stories, and is the ultimate polymath – he is an expert at everything.

I am sure we all know someone like this. When we're having a casual chat with our friends about the hundred years' war in **Jean d'Arcy** the movie, Mr. Little says, "Actually, the war happened between 1337 – 1453 AD in Europe, which (and he chuckling clears his throat) clearly is more than one hundred years, but because of certain periods of cease-fire during the war's Edwardian, Caroline, and Lancastrian phases…" and he goes on and on like a speaking Wikipedia turning the conversation into a monologue and evidence of how smart he is. The people around him might tolerate him (since he is the lil'boss, or simply to be courteous), but his likability factor decreases with every historical date he mentions.

I am not saying that being smart or knowledgeable is bad. If somebody is curious about something and you know the answer that is great. You'll grow significantly in that person's eyes. But if you want to push your knowledge onto someone else when they are not asking just to prove how much stuff you know, it might be counterproductive.

The problem

Overconfidence is another manifestation of low self-confidence. Overconfident people want to prevent judgment and failure by taking the first step and deterring people with a knowledgeable attitude. However, truly confident people do not feel the need to prove themselves. They can be smart and assertive without being pushy and running over other people's confidence. Self-confidence is not the same as being arrogant, knowing it all, or easily writing people off. Overconfidence is an emotionally unintelligent behavior that, although it might seem like genuine confidence, only serves to cover up deep-rooted insecurities.

In addition, the action itself is counterintuitive. Usually overconfident people thirst for others' admiration and acceptance, just like attention-seeking people from the previous chapter. However, they, instead of baking cookies, try to gain admiration by undertaking an air of superiority. However, they will win the sympathy of very few people, if any, because nobody likes to feel inferior. In most cases, humble people with great knowledge are admired at the level overconfident people want to be.

Do not get me wrong, overconfident people are not bad or stupid. They are lost in their own emotional insecurity that manifests itself in this way. They should not be judged or hated more than people whose emotional outbursts are much more likable or socially appropriate. They need help.

The benefit of choosing to be humble instead of boastful

Humble people are not afraid to keep their thoughts and knowledge to themselves. They do not feel the burning need to correct others either.

I read a story in Dale Carnegie's book, **How to Win Friends and Influence People**. The point of the story was that Carnegie's friend went to an event with one of his students. They met somebody there who attributed a quote to the wrong author. Carnegie's friend did not correct him, even though he (and his student) knew it was incorrect. After the person who misquoted left, the student asked the following question:

> - Why didn't you tell him he was wrong?
> - You think I should have. What benefit would there have been? Now we have the benevolence of this man. If I corrected him, even though I am right, I would have lost his good intentions. When it comes to minor issues like this, it is better to stay silent and keep one's good opinion than to prove you are right and win the argument.

I could not agree more! Self-confident people are not in need of constant showdowns to prove themselves. They do not need to run over other people's self-esteem to avoid their limiting beliefs. They appreciate friendly moments instead because it brings them closer to feeling appreciated. I would not say that they do not enjoy expressing their knowledge from time to time, but they are not bullies or polymaths. They only speak when they are asked.

The solution

A person lacking confidence always leaves small clues. Unlike the overconfident, unapproachable air, these people have a hard time admitting mistakes. They hardly ever apologize, and the boasting tendencies are among the many signs of low confidence.

Boasting looks like confidence on the surface, but as I mentioned before, confident people do not feel the need to brag. Only those who do are trying to convince themselves of their own worth.

Do you worry about looking incompetent in the eyes of others? Do you have trouble admitting your shortcomings? Do you hesitate to accept other people's advice or opinions because you think they are not smart enough?

If your answer was yes to the questions above, you may want to consider developing your EQ (Emotional Quotient) with different techniques, and using your knowledge and expertise to become truly likable and successful.

How can you defeat overconfidence?

1. Honesty

Think back to all the occasions when you were acting with an air of superiority and look for the reasons why. Admit that you were acting boastfully or like a polymath because… you were afraid that others knew it better and so you wanted to make the first smart step, or you wanted some appreciation or… whatever your reasons were. Do not forget which situations make you act overconfident. Is it a specific person, a certain event…?

Then be mindful of it, and when you face the situation next time and you feel like the boasting monster is about to get out, pull it back. Listen instead of talking, try to understand others, and try to get backstage as an observer. If people ask, answer the question. If they ask more, say more. You will see how much your overall perception will change just by taking it a little bit easier.

2. Do not compare yourself to others

The need to be overconfident roots in your negative comparison with others. Sometimes overconfidence pairs up with recklessness and it drives you to engage in situations that you are prepared for just because you think **if that fool Jimmy can do it flawlessly so can I.** However, maybe Jimmy did, let us say paraglide many times in his life. He invested many hours in mastering this craft. You cannot be as good as Jimmy the first time you go paragliding. Know your limits.

3.   Give credit to positive criticism

First look at who says it, then listen to what they have to say. However, if you generally struggle to accept criticism, start with criticism from people you truly look up to and respect. Ask for their honest feedback. This does not mean that critics are always right. However, there is a possibility that they are. In addition, just for the sake of practicing to hear out another person's opinion of you, you should listen to him or her.

4.   Take time to reflect on events when your overconfident attitude didn't do you any good

When you see your actions without bias, it will help you to create a realistic picture of your actions. Find out where you went wrong, and think about how you can approach the situation differently next time. When you find the skills and qualities, you need to work on, take time and improve them.

5.   Don't kill what you already have

Try to look at your overconfidence issues with an analytical perspective. If you become too harsh with yourself, the whole process of overcoming overconfidence can result in a loss of confidence.

Keep your knowledge, your spirit, whatever you feel proud of and whatever makes you feel comfortable. Be mindful of them. Use them at the right time with the right people in the right amount.

Mike Bray

Chapter 2. Uncovering the Roots of Your Social Anxiety

Do you want to find out what has been causing your social anxiety? If you do, then you will need a sheet of paper, a pen, a quiet place where no one would disturb you for a while, and maybe a cup of hot tea for comfort.

First, ask yourself, what could be the cause of your problems with social anxiety? Begin with your family. Do you have any relatives who may have or have had social anxiety?

It cannot be helped that genes play a role in the development of an anxiety disorder, although it should not be considered as the only factor. Social anxiety, for one, is typically triggered by an experience in the environment and most especially among peers. If you do have family members with an anxiety disorder, it is highly advised that you consult a health professional regarding the symptoms you are experiencing with relation to your anxiety.

The Influence of Home
Aside from your family history regarding anxiety, the next thing to consider is whether your parents, guardians, or other family members had influenced you to becoming socially anxious, whether it is them

modeling the behaviors or having a parenting style that encourages –knowingly or unknowingly– such behavior. Were they overprotective? Were they too controlling? Were they inconsistent in their parenting style?

While this should not lead to anyone blaming their parents for their social anxiety, reflecting on the kind of home environment you had as a child can help you uncover the reason behind your fears. It is important to remember, however, that parenting is one of the most difficult and challenging lifelong tasks because there is no perfect way to raise children with different personalities.

That said, children might grow up to have social anxiety if they are raised in a home where the parents overprotected them, controlled them too much, or were erratic in their parenting style.

Overprotective parents, for instance, would cause their child to be less exposed to frustrations, the feeling of being anxious or afraid, or failure. This will make such life experiences even more daunting to them for they have not been given the opportunity to overcome them in the past.

Controlling parents, on the other hand, do not foster independence and in fact would instill constant anxiety in their children due to their rules and standards. Many children who grew up in this environment tend to become either rebellious or too dependent on others.

On the other hand, parents with unpredictable parental

behavior are the ones who would be kind and loving one day, and angry and violent the next. Children raised in this erratic parenting style have the tendency to develop a lack of trust towards other people in general. They are also likely to develop anxiety because they feel as if they do not have any control over their lives.

With all these in mind, would you say that your home environment as a child played a role in your social anxiety? If you think that none of these would describe your situation, then perhaps we can look into the third set of factors, which is the environment beyond the home.

Negative Social Situations
In the age of information and the internet, the world has become even smaller than before. Likewise, we have become even busier, filling our days with tons of task regardless of whether many of them are truly beneficial to our wellbeing or not. Therefore, it has become increasingly common for people to feel so stressed out that they become anxious in many given situations.

Many experts of the study of anxiety have identified three specific situations that can lead to the fear of certain social situations. Let us discuss more about them so that you can determine which one has contributed the most to your social anxiety: An event in which one becomes the subject of uncalled for rejections, judgment, and/or criticism by peers is perhaps the most common social situation that triggers social anxiety. Even the most confident person in the world becomes vulnerable to self-doubt and constant worry over one's appearance, skills, talents, social background, et cetera, if their confidence is trampled by others.

For example, let us say you were unexpectedly invited to perform a song in front of a big party. You have always been confident with your voice and you have in fact won a few contests. However, in this unexpected situation, you were somehow unprepared and so halfway through the song; you forgot the rest of the lyrics. As the people laughed at and teased you for forgetting, you considered it such an embarrassment that you lost confidence in yourself.

The second anxiety-causing event is a traumatic experience, especially if it was a life-threatening or horrifying one. An act of terrorism, a natural disaster, violence, or a horrific accident could lead to severe anxiety problems.

Here is an example of how a traumatic experience could lead to social anxiety: let us say Bob was at a public speaking event when the main speaker was suddenly gunned down. The crowd turned into a raging stampede that left Bob severely injured and traumatized. Ever since then, he always avoided large crowds and any event where there is public speaking involved.

The third event is one in which a person has experienced an unforeseen threat, causing the person to lose a sense of security and stability. This may be regarded as a somewhat lighter experience as compared with a traumatic one, nevertheless it is still quite damaging to one's sense of self-confidence.

For instance, let us say you used to be relatively well-off and could afford anything you wanted. You had many equally rich friends and you always attended major social gatherings together. Then, one day you lost all the money because you were unexpectedly laid off and what little savings you had had run out. Because of this unforeseen circumstance, you begin to avoid any social situations with people who were with you when you still had money.

Which of these scenarios could you relate to the most? You do not have to delve deeply into the memory of that experience to know it was the one that caused your social anxiety. After all, that was in the past and no longer a part of your reality. What matters now is that you want to overcome your anxiety towards specific social situations. That way, you can enjoy a truly meaningful life.

Moving towards Acceptance
At this point, you probably already know what caused your social anxiety. If you still do not, then you might want to seek the help of a licensed therapist to help you uproot the underlying problem. However, if you can clearly state why you have social anxiety, then the next step is to accept that it is all in the past.

To help you with that, answer the following questions as honestly as you can. You may choose to write down your response or you can say it out loud to yourself. Here are the questions:

- **Do I blame myself for my shyness?**

- Do I purposefully want to be shy and anxious whenever I find myself in (a specific social situation)?

- If my best friend struggled with social anxiety, how can I help them?

- If I continue to worry and be fearful towards (a specific social situation), will my health, mood, and overall wellbeing improve?

- Am I capable of overcoming my social anxiety? What will happen if I do overcome it?

- If I could channel the energy I would normally spend on worrying and thinking negatively on something else, what would it be?

Take your time in answering these questions, especially when you notice that your mind tends to shift its focus back towards negative thoughts. If your negative thought patterns seem too overwhelming, however, then you will be able to progress well with the help of a mental health professional. He or she can guide you through the best therapy that will help you overcome social anxiety and your negative thought patterns.

Identifying the Intensity of your Social Anxiety
If you tend to feel anxious towards a variety of social

situations, and if you are not sure of where to begin in terms of overcoming your social anxiety, then it is best to have a professional conduct a clinical interview to help you specify your problem. To help prepare you for this interview, this section provides you with some of the commonly-asked questions. Try to answer them on your own using the following intensity scale:

Fear Scale

0 to 1–None

2 to 4–Mild

5 to 6–Moderate

7 to 8–Extreme

9 to 10–Very Extreme

Anxiety Scale

0 to 1–Never Avoid

2 to 4–Rarely Avoid

5 to 6–Occasionally Avoid

7 to 8–Often Avoid

9 to 10–Always Avoid

Now, based on the scales, you can rate your levels of fear and avoidance in each of the following social situations:

Social Situation	Fear	Avoidance
Starting a conversation with an acquaintance		
Asking someone to go out with you		
Having company over at your house		
Introducing yourself to others		
Being introduced to people you have not met before		
Talking to a friend over the telephone		
Talking to a stranger over the telephone		
Sharing an idea or personal opinion to an acquaintance		
Sharing an idea or		

personal opinion to a group		
Being interviewed for a job position		
Returning a purchase to a shop		
Standing up for yourself (when someone is being unreasonable to you)		
Saying "no" to a request		
Presenting a report at work		
Speaking up in a meeting or class		
Sharing a speech or making a toast at a social gathering		
Singing, dancing, or performing something in front of other people		
Sharing a meal with other people		
Sharing a public bathroom with other people		

Writing or typing something with other people reading what you are writing/typing		
Making a mistake in front of others		
Shopping in a high-traffic store		

You can also add other social situations and then note down the corresponding rates you want to give them. After that, you can highlight which of them have the highest scores in terms of fear, avoidance, and both. That way, you can immediately identify which social situations trigger your social anxiety. Hold on to this information because it will serve an important purpose later on.

Now, aside from anxiety-inducing social situations, another factor that contributes to your feelings of anxiety would be the traits of other people. Most socially-anxious people are not immediately aware that they start to feel highly uncomfortable around people with certain traits, which is why it is important to know which ones affect you the most.

Here is the scale to use in rating:
Discomfort Scale
0 to 1–No Discomfort
2 to 4–Mild Discomfort
5 to 6–Moderate Discomfort
7 to 8–Extreme Discomfort

9 to 10–Very Extreme Discomfort

The following table shows the qualities of other people.
Based on the scale above, rate your level of discomfort
towards each given quality and then add some notes to
specify the reasons for your ratings, if necessary:

Qualities of the Other Person	Level of Discomfort	Notes
Biological sex of the person (same sex, opposite sex)		
Gender identity of the person (heterosexual, homosexual, bisexual, etc.)		
Age of the other person (older, younger, same age)		

Relationship (single,dating someone, married, separated, divorced, widowed, etc.)		
Physical attractiveness of the other person		
The appearance of the other person (such as if the person is well-dressed, etc.)		
Ethnic background or nationality of the other person		
The level of confidence in the behavior of the other person (highly self-confident,		

moderately self-confident, not self-confident, etc.)		
The aggressive or abrasive behavior of the other person		
The charm or good sense of humor of the other person		
The financial stability of the other person		

Aside from these qualities, you can add some more that are likely to pop into mind while you are answering this. Once you have given a rating to all of them, you can then highlight the qualities of the other person that make you feel most uncomfortable, because these shed a light to the sources of your social anxiety.

Relationship Aspect with the Other Person	Level of Discomfort	Notes
The other person is very close to you (a partner, family member, close friend, etc.)		
The other person is not close to you but you know each other's names (an acquaintance, a co-worker, etc.)		
The other person is not close to you and neither of you knows each other's names (a store clerk, a stranger, etc.)		
The other person and you have a history of conflict that has been resolved (a former rival, enemy, etc.)		

The other person and you have a history of conflict that has not been resolved (a current rival, enemy, etc.)		
The social or professional position of the other person is higher than yours (your employer, supervisor, team leader, etc.)		
The social or professional position of the other person is the same as yours (your co-worker, teammate, etc.)		
The social or professional position of the other person is lower than yours (your employee, supervisee, etc.)		

The next step is to determine your level of discomfort towards the kind of relationship you have with other people. Using the same Discomfort scale, rate the following aspects and again take note of any specificities:

Next, you are going to rate your level of discomfort for the following aspects of a social situation. As with the other categories, you can also add your own specific aspects and rate them accordingly.

Aspects of a Social Situation	Level of Discomfort	Notes
The level of formality of the social situation (formal, business formal, semi-formal, casual, etc.)		
The lighting of the venue (bright light, natural light (outdoors in the daytime), dim light, etc.)		
The number of people in the social situation (one other person, a few people, a large group, a crowd, etc.)		

Your physical position during the social situation (standing, seated, lying down, etc.)		
The activity required or recommended during the social situation (eating, writing, talking, watching a movie, etc.)		
The presence of certain food, beverages, or other substances in the social situation (alcohol, cigarettes, drugs, etc.)		
The length of time of the social situation (about 15 minutes, 30 minutes, 1 hour, more than an hour, etc.)		

After you have given much thought to rating the different levels of intensity regarding the various aspects of a social situation, you are most likely able to pinpoint where your social anxiety is coming from. Knowing these details is highly important to your progress because it then leads to acknowledgement and acceptance of your problem.

Now, you would be glad to know that there is a healthy, simple, and easily accessible solution to overcome social anxiety, and it is called Mindfulness. Whether you are battling social anxiety on your own, or you are going through therapy to overcome it, you can definitely apply mindfulness. Turn to the next chapter to learn more about how it can help you.

Chapter 3. How Mindfulness Can Help You Overcome Social Anxiety

If you are the kind of person who is up to date on the latest mind-body wellness buzzwords and trends, then you must have already heard about Mindfulness. It has become such a big movement that even multinational companies such as Google and Procter & Gamble are promoting the practice of Mindfulness among their employees as it helps boost productivity and overall wellbeing.

In this particular chapter, you will read about Mindfulness as it is defined in ancient Buddhism, by its modern-day, secular supporters, and as it relates to social anxiety.

What Mindfulness Means
In general terms, Mindfulness is defined as the trait of conscientiously paying full attention to one's present moment experiences. These experiences include what is happening within you (such as your breath, your thoughts, and so on) as well as what is happening around you (or the sights, sounds, smells, and so on in your environment). Formal mindfulness practice involves meditation, which helps train the mind to become more mindful. Informal mindfulness practice, on the other

hand, is one in which a person would pay full attention to what he or she is doing at that moment, such as while he is walking, eating, washing the dishes, and so on.

Unfortunately, many people still are not sure of what Mindfulness really means. Some think it is boring and pointless, while others think it is just another fad. However, Mindfulness is not a new concept, but one that has been practiced for almost three thousand years by ancient Buddhists in order to achieve clarity and deep concentration during meditation.

Mindfulness in Ancient Buddhism
The term mindfulness itself was drawn from the word *sati* (which literally means"memory") from the ancient Prakrit language of Pali, which is the scriptural and liturgical language of Theravada Buddhism. The scholar Thomas William Rhys Davids was the first one to coin this term, and explained that it references the Buddhist principle of constantly maintaining presence of mind. Some of the other English translations of *sati*are"awareness," "self-recollection"(said the Buddhist teacher Jack Kornfield),"retention,"and"inspection"(according to Herbert Guenther, a German Buddhist philosopher and professor).

The reason why Buddhists practice mindfulness is that they consider it as an antidote to delusion, greed, and hatred. Through mindfulness, their perception and comprehension of what is taking place become clearer. This is because the ancient Buddhists believe that the body and mind are made up of the Five Aggregates (or *khandhas*, in Pali), which are as follows: material form, feelings, perceptions, volition, and sensory consciousness.

- The first aggregate, Material Form, is made up of the physical components of the body (in other words, the organs) as well as all external matter that ceaselessly move to and from the body (such as the air we breathe).

- The second aggregate, Feelings, involves all emotions, whether neutral, pleasant, or unpleasant.

- The third, Perceptions, is described as the awareness of the different features–colors, textures, shapes, and so on–of the object that is being perceived.

- The fourth aggregate, Volition, is defined as the verbal, psychological, and physical behavior the person chooses to do as influenced by the former three aggregates.

- The fifth and final aggregate, Sensory Consciousness, is the sum of all the previous aggregates. It is how the

person comprehends the thought that arises in his or her mind or the input detected by any of his or her five senses (sight, hearing, tasting, smelling, and touch). A person's Sensory Consciousness is heavily influenced by his or her memories of previous experiences as well as conditioned attitudes towards the object.

According to Buddhists, lack of understanding of the five aggregates triggers suffering, pain, and dissatisfaction because it causes a person to cling to things that are actually not permanent. That is because Buddhists believe the five aggregates arise and cease from moment to moment and are, therefore, impermanent. Ancient Buddhist texts even state that the Buddha compared material form to foam, feelings to bubbles, perceptions to mirages, volition to the plantain trunk (which grows and then rots), and sensory consciousness to an illusion.

Now, you might be thinking that all of these Buddhist beliefs sound quite far-fetched. However, all these make a lot of sense if you compare the Five Aggregates with social anxiety, specifically your anxiety-provoking thoughts and attitudes towards a given social situation. The first two aggregates represent the physical and emotional symptoms of anxiety. The third aggregate would refer to how you perceive the given social situation. The fourth aggregate represents the kind of behavior you would resort to in reaction to your social anxiety, such as by making sure to avoid the social situation. Finally, your sensory consciousness would cause you to believe that you do and always will have social anxiety, even though this is not true.

On the other hand, if a Buddhist chooses to practice mindfulness, meditation, and the Noble Eightfold Path as taught by the Buddha, he or she would be able to break free from the Five Aggregates. In the context of social anxiety, this means you would no longer associate your social consciousness with having social anxiety if you become more mindful of your physical and emotional reaction, perceptions, and behavior towards the given social situation. In short, you would come to accept that all sensory experiences, feelings, and thought are impermanent.

Modern-Day Mindfulness for Mental Health

Nowadays, anyone can practice it regardless of whether he or she believes in Buddhist doctrine or not. Even western medicine promotes the practice of mindfulness as a form of complementary therapy to those dealing with chronic pain and mental illnesses such as depression. Psychologists A.M. Haynes and G. Feldman explained that mindfulness is a technique that can help a person overcome the strategy of emotion avoidance and emotional over-engagement, both of which can lead to mental disorders.

In addition, clinical psychologists recognize a two-component mindfulness model to explain the role of mindfulness in helping to overcome a mental disorder. The first component involves the person to regulate his or her own attention so that it is focused on"immediate experience"(what is going on in the present moment, including one's thoughts, feelings, and sensations). The second component involves the person adopting an attitude of acceptance, openness, and curiosity towards this immediate experience. Psychologists also explicitly state that the person should avoid attempting to reach a specific state, such as relaxation, because there should be no end goal to mindfulness.

Mindfulness-Based Cognitive Therapy or MBCT, is one such type of psychological therapy that employs mindfulness as a means of preventing relapse of Major Depressive Disorder and other forms of depression. It is based on the theory that those who had been diagnosed with depression are likely to relapse due to automatic negative thoughts. It is for this reason that MBCT is geared towards helping the person become fully aware of his or her thoughts and feelings, and to accept them without clinging or reacting to them. Therefore, instead of reacting to these negative thoughts, he or she would be more reflective of them. Multiple studies, including one published in the 2004 issue of *Journal of Consulting and Clinical Psychology,* support the effectiveness of MBCT in reducing relapse by approximately 50 percent (among people who experienced at least three episodes of depression).

Acceptance and Commitment Therapy, or ACT, is another psychological therapy approach that applies mindfulness techniques to help people become in tune with the present moment, to be more open towards unpleasant feelings so as to not overreact or avoid them.

ACT has six principles that are geared towards helping others become more"psychologically flexible."These principles are as follows:

- *Cognitive defusion, which involves learning strategies to minimize one's tendency to reify emotions, thoughts, memories, and images*
- *Acceptance, which is letting thoughts arise and then fade away without engaging with them*
- *Contact with the present moment, which is to become aware, with*

curiosity and openness, of the here and now

- *Observing the self, which is accessing the"transcendent sense of self,"or the unchanging, continuous stream of consciousness*

- *Values, which involves discovering the core values or what matters the most to one's"true self"*

- *Committed action, which is setting goals based on the values of one's true self and then working towards accomplishing them*

According to psychotherapists who administer ACT, many problems–including social anxiety– is triggered by four concepts, which are: Fusion with your thoughts, Evaluation of experience, Avoidance of your experience, and Reason-giving of your behavior. They use the acronym FEAR to help their patients remember these triggers. As for overcoming them, one must ACT, or rather: Accept one's reactions and be present, choose a valued direction, and Take action.

Aside from these two modern-day mindfulness approaches to combat mental issues such as social anxiety, psychiatrists offer plenty of other options. You can talk to a trusted health professional about them so that you will know which one best suits you.

Now, as you are more familiar with the concept of mindfulness as it relates to social anxiety, it is safe to assume that you have a clearer picture of how it can help you overcome your problem. In the remaining chapters, you will learn how to cope with your nerves in social situations, deal with your fearful thoughts, and move towards having more compassion towards yourself.

Chapter 4. Mindfulness Strategies to Overcome Anxiety-Triggered Thoughts and Behavior

Mindfulness becomes much easier when you gain a deeper understanding of your own thought processes. This can be achieved by broadening your knowledge and experiences on how the mind works, in general.

Through the years, mental health experts have been able to research on and collect a vast body of knowledge about the thought patterns of socially-anxious people. In their studies, they were able to pinpoint the common reasons behind anxiety-triggered thoughts and behavior. This chapter will show you these commonalities so that you can reflect as to whether you also experience them yourself.

Acknowledging Your Anxiety-Triggering Thoughts
As what you have read in the previous chapters, mindless thought patterns can cause to aggravate any feelings of anxiety you may have towards a given social situation. For instance, if you believe the other people at the party will judge you for not being financially stable or wearing nice, expensive clothes, then it is only natural for you to feel anxious.

Most of the time, however, our thoughts and beliefs about what would happen in any situation, are not based on reality. We actually tend to exaggerate them with our negative thought patterns, even though we know that nothing good will really come of it.

If you are having trouble identifying your own negative thought patterns that have been triggering your social anxiety, then you can apply the following mindfulness strategy to bring them forth. You can use either a pen and paper or a sound recorder to take note of your responses to the following self-reflective questions. After which, you can then read or listen to your answers to learn more about how your mind works during times when you feel socially anxious.

Here are the steps to follow:

Step 1: Find a quiet, secure, and comfortable place where you can spend some time alone without anyone to disturb you. Once you are there, find a nice spot where you can write or record your thoughts into words.

Step 2: Begin by thinking of a social situation that causes you to feel anxious. If you wish, you may close your eyes and visualize in your mind all the different elements of that situation, from the sights, the sounds, the smells, and the overall atmosphere.

Step 3: As you begin to feel the familiar, albeit milder, physical and emotional symptoms of anxiety as provoked by the vision, notice how you react to the situation. Become fully aware of each symptom that transpires. Do not attempt to judge or think too much about the symptoms, but simply acknowledge them.

For instance, if you notice your heart beating faster, say,"my heart is beating faster right now."

After acknowledging all of the symptoms, you may choose to take note of them before you move on to the next step.

Step 4: Now, ask yourself,"What is it about this social situation that scares me?"Acknowledge every single thought inside your mind in response to this question. You may say it out loud into your recorder or write it down on your sheet of paper.

Step 5: Move on to the next question, which is,"What might the other person or people in the situation be thinking about me?"Again, record your reaction.

Step 6: Ask yourself,"Is it so important for the other person or people to think of me in a positive way? Why is it so important?" Take note of your response.

Step 7: Ask yourself,"How will I behave or react in this given situation? Will I avoid it or not? Why is this my reaction?"After that, ask yourself,"What are my expectations of this social situation? Why do I think this negative thing will happen?"Record all your answers.

Step 8: Consider the situation wherein your negative expectations of the social situation would actually take place. Then, ask yourself,"What will I do if what I expect to happen in the social situation actually does happen? What will happen next after that?"Take note of your response to these questions as well as any other beliefs or thoughts that are aggravating your anxiety.

After doing this exercise, allow yourself some time to relax first and enjoy the things you take comfort in before you review your answers. This will refresh you and help you approach your responses in a more objective and mindful way.

Be careful not to criticize your responses or reflect on whether they are exaggerated or not as you read or listen to them. Rather, they are there simply to help you become more aware of your own thoughts and feelings, particularly those related to your social anxiety. It is also important to remember that you are much more than these anxious thoughts and feelings, and that you can always change if you so choose.

Becoming Aware of your Anxiety-Triggered Behavior

Anxiety is usually followed by the desire to act upon it in order to reduce its intensity. While there are hundreds, if not thousands, of possibilities as to how you would behave in reaction to social anxiety, mental health experts have identified three common types of anxiety-triggered behaviors, which are discussed below.

Perhaps after reading through each type, you might want to also reflect on whether you can relate to one or more of them. Therefore, you will probably want to have a pen and paper ready to take note of your thoughts.

Social Anxiey

Avoidance

The most common behavioral response to social anxiety is to avoid the situation. Avoiding the social situation may give you instant relief, but it will never remove your anxiety.

Here are some common examples of avoidance:

- When the phone is ringing and you muffle it with a pillow or put it on silent mode after it stops

- When you turn down offers to do an interview or present a report

- When you make up excuses to avoid attending a social event

- When you purposefully choose a different, albeit less convenient, route to a destination in order to avoid a certain person or group of people

Have you ever avoided certain social situations before due to your anxiety? Browse through your notes (especially the ones from Chapter 2) and think of other situations that you have avoided in the past as well as your reasons for doing so.

Constant Reassurance Seeking A strong desire to appear in a certain way to other people is common among many of those with social anxiety. Therefore, they constantly seek reassurance to ensure that they still have these qualities.

Some examples of constant reassurance seeking are described below:

- **When you ask your friend or partner if you are fat, unattractive, and so on**

- **When you constantly check the mirror to make sure that your hair, outfit, clothes, etc., are perfect**

- **When you post too many pictures of yourself online and then check if anyone approves of them (such as how many"likes"it gets on Facebook, etc.)**

While there is nothing wrong with seeking reassurance every now and then, the confidence of socially-anxious people in a given situation rely too much on it. The problem lies in their belief that something is wrong with them if they do not have such qualities. It also negatively supports anxiety-provoking thoughts such as worrying about how other people see them or think about them.

Moreover, their peers and family might grow exhausted from having to give them reassurance constantly, especially since they are being compelled to make judgments.

It can be difficult to detect whether you seek constant reassurance, especially if you have been unaware of it. However, you can start to become more mindful of your thought patterns so that you can watch for any signs of this defense mechanism for social anxiety. You can also reflect on certain situations wherein you resorted to this tactic and then try to consider your underlying reasons for doing so.

Overcompensation
When a person with social anxiety believes he or she has certain flaws, he or she would find a way to overcompensate in order to hide them, even though most of the time these flaws are purely perceived by their imagination.

Take a look at the following situational examples of overcompensation:

- Over-preparing for a report or presentation, such as by memorizing word-for-word even though it is not necessary
- Rehearsing what to ask and how to respond to a future conversation with a date or friend

- Trying so hard to be entertaining, charming, etc., even though you feel uncomfortable and unnatural doing so because you fear people would think you are boring

- Putting on too much makeup, wearing flashy clothes, etc., to hide a physical feature you are insecure about

Just like the constant reassurance seeking defense mechanism, overcompensation can be hard to detect especially if you have convinced yourself that such behavior is simply a part of your identity. However, by paying attention to how you really feel and what you truly think about these behaviors, you can overcome your insecurities and become truly confident in yourself.

Now that you have a better understanding of how your mind works, the next step is for you to create a series of steps towards mindfully responding–rather than merely reacting– to your social anxiety.

While no one can truly predict or control the kinds of thoughts that pop up in our heads, we do have the power to question them and interpret them. By interpreting your anxious thoughts in a curious, compassionate, and open way, you can reprogram your flight or fight response towards a given social situation.

Mindfulness Techniques to Enhance Self-Esteem in Social Situations

We all experience having low self-esteem every now and then, but in people with social anxiety, it is experienced almost every day. It becomes especially low during moments when they are about to face the social situation which they fear the most.

It can be comforting to simply avoid these social situations, but the healing process only starts when one mindfully reflects on the underlying cause. Why do these social situations cause you anxiety? How can you regain your self-esteem now that you know of these triggers?

You alone will be able to answer these questions. To help you discover them, you can use the following mindfulness techniques as your guide:
Become Mindful of your Reactions

Mindfulness is about enjoying the present moment in an open, non-judgmental way. However, mindfulness can also be interpreted as remembering things in a compassionate and curious way. Looking into how you reacted to given social situations in the past can help you find out why they caused you to feel stressed and scared. Then, you can use these discoveries to help you regain self-esteem and overcome your social anxiety bit by bit.

Here are the steps to do this:
Step 1: Find a quiet, comfortable place where you can sit

and write down your thoughts for a while. Bring a pen and paper with you.

Step 2: As you sit with pen and paper in hand, close your eyes and focus on your breath for a few minutes. Let your mind be filled with nothing but thoughts of the sensations you feel as you breathe.

Step 3: When you are ready, try to call to memory a time when you felt unconfident during a social situation. Allow your mind to picture out the details as vividly as you can, including your reaction to the situation. After that, slowly open your eyes and write down the details on the sheet of paper.

Here is an example: Last Monday, my old high school classmate invited me to a lunch gathering with our other classmates. At first, I could not say no, but I was able to find an excuse and so I told her that I could not make it. I was so relieved afterwards.

Step 4: Describe the sensations and emotions you felt for not being confident in that social situation. Try to recall the thoughts that crossed your mind during that time. Then, write down everything you can remember.

For example: I pretended to smile when she told me to attend the gathering. However, deep inside I was already thinking about how nice she still looks while I'm starting to get heavy around the edges. I had seen on Facebook how amazing her little family is and how they always travel during the summers. It makes me feel bad and I worry that my other classmates might ask me about my life during the gathering. I remember my heart racing and my head pounding at the thought… so, I had to say no.

After this short exercise, give yourself some time to breathe and relax before you read through your notes. Be mindful, compassionate, and non-judgmental towards yourself as you read, because what you wrote is raw and honest, and serves as groundwork for your progress.

Recognize and Let Go of Assumptions

Incorrect assumptions can eat away your self-esteem quickly unless you catch them as they come to mind. However, it is difficult to step out of your assumptions once they are there, so the better way is to equip yourself with the knowledge and mindfulness to prevent them or counteract them in a healthy way. Socially-anxious people make five main types of assumptions, namely Overestimation, Personalization, Catastrophizing, Mind Reading, and Black and White Mentality. Read through each type and then reflect as to whether your anxious thoughts fall under any of them.

Overestimation
Overestimation is when you make an assumption that something is highly likely to happen, or that what you think the other person is thinking is most likely true.

For instance, someone who is scared of meeting new people might assume that in the next acquaintance party he or she is going to make a bad impression. Another example is when a socially-anxious person who does not think he or she is attractive enough would assume that the people at the party would find him or her to be unattractive.

Here are example statements of Overestimation:

- Now that my partner has left me, I am certainly going to die alone and depressed.

- My family thinks I am a disappointment.

- My friend only feels sorry for me because I could not find a good job.

Personalization

This type of assumption is when you take a negative situation personally, in that you believe it to be your fault when in fact, there are plenty of other factors that contribute to it.

For instance, if you see some people fall asleep during your speech, you would immediately assume that you are not a good speaker. However, it is also possible that the topic was just not something the audience could relate to, or that it was the time of the day when people are generally sleepy, or that there are still people who are listening intently to you. Unless you become mindful that you are personalizing the incident, you could end up avoiding similar social situations in the future.

Here are examples of Personalization statements:

- After talking for only a few minutes, my new co-worker excused herself from the conversation. I guess that makes me a pretty boring conversationalist.

- My seatmate looks agitated. She must be really mad at me for sitting next to her.

- That guy across the room is staring at me. He must be disgusted by my outfit right now.

Catastrophizing

This is the assumption that something terrible is about to happen to a social situation. While we all do experience unfortunate incidents in social situations from time to time, such as embarrassing ourselves in front of others or committing some sort of social faux pas, some of us can just shrug it off and not keep the memory of it from allowing us to have a good time with others.

In many socially-anxious people, however, this thought is often generalized, so much so that they think it will happen in all future social situations.

Here are some example statements of Catastrophizing:

- It would be a catastrophe if I sing off-key on stage.

- I cannot imagine how terrible it would be if they see how bad my skin is at the reunion.

- I will only make a fool of myself if I volunteer, I am sure of it!

Black and White Mentality

This type of assumption is when a person judges anything as either perfect or unacceptable. A socially-anxious person would consider him or herself to either be perfect or face the consequences of rejection. It is for this reason that many perfectionists avoid social situations in which they might be judged for their"flaws."

In addition, socially-anxious people tend to use should statements most of the time, such as *should, must, ought to, always,* and *never.* For instance, they would say,"I should never make any mistakes," "I must never be laughed at, or else I will become the unwitting class clown," "I ought to look perfect whenever my ex sees me, or else!"or"I never bother the teacher with my stupid questions."All these lead to unrealistic expectations for themselves and others.

Here are some example statements of Black and White Mentality:

- If I do not perform flawlessly during this demonstration, I will fail miserably and embarrass myself in front of the judges.

- I do not want people to see me crying because it is a sign of weakness.

- There is no point attending the party when I do not even have nice clothes to wear. Everyone will think I'm shabby.

What do you think of these types of assumptions? What do you think is the impact of these assumptions on your self-esteem? Do you think you have committed any one of them?

If you could not stop yourself from entertaining assumptions, you can use mindfulness as your filter to keep them from affecting your self-esteem. Start by paying attention to your thoughts and then identify whether they are facts or mere assumptions.

For instance, if you notice yourself thinking, "I am going to embarrass myself in front of these people, for sure!" Stop and think, "Is this a fact, or am I simply assuming this? How helpful is this assumption to me? Will my performance improve if I worry about it?"

Continue to be mindful and you will soon come to realize that the only thing that is keeping you from becoming truly confident is your own mind.

Stop Making Negative Comparisons

We humans have the tendency to evaluate ourselves constantly, and a way of doing that is by comparing ourselves with others. We cannot blame ourselves for doing so, especially since most societies openly compare people. Take, for example, the fact that many schools would rank the children from highest to lowest based on their test scores, or that beauty pageants would reveal who the judges think to be the smartest, prettiest, most well dressed, etc., among the contestants.

While a little competition is part of what makes life so exciting, it is an altogether different story if you approach it in a negative way. Many socially-anxious people tend to compare themselves with someone who is not entirely relevant to them. For instance, it would do no one any good to compare their own physical appearance with that of a supermodel on a magazine cover, because it will do nothing but create feelings of inadequacy. Sadly, many people are not mindful enough of this bad habit, which is why they tend to suffer from their insecurities on a daily basis.

According to research, the habit of comparing oneself to others is different for socially-anxious people compared with those who do not suffer from social anxiety. What they do is they would more frequently compare themselves with those whom they believe to be"better"than them. Naturally, this would constantly make them feel bad about themselves.

For a moment, stop and reflect on whether you have been comparing yourself to others, and whether you believe them to be"better" than you. Reflect on those times when you did that and what led you to do so. Write down all the thoughts that cross your mind. Then, read all you have written and consider the advantages and disadvantages of comparing yourself to others. Perhaps you will notice that while it motivates you to do better, it also causes you to resent others or be unfair towards yourself.

If you want to end the cycle of comparing yourself with others, here are the steps to take:
Step 1: Become mindful of your thoughts when you notice other people. Do you compare your own strengths and weaknesses with theirs? How does it make you feel while doing that? Notice all the sensations, emotions, and thoughts that cross your mind as you compare.

Step 2: After becoming fully aware that you are automatically comparing yourself with others, gently direct your attention towards your breath. This is a way to shift your focus from these thoughts towards the present moment.

Step 3: Call to mind everything you are grateful for in life as of the moment. Focus on what you now have in life, whether it is your personal strengths, your relationships with others, or an accomplishment you have made, no matter how big or small. Spend time expressing your gratitude towards your life right now.

It will not be easy to draw your focus away from

thoughts of comparing yourself to others, especially when you are facing them in a social situation. However, by practicing these steps whenever you notice the urge to do so, you will be able to break the habit of comparing. In turn, you will have nothing but gratitude and confidence in your life and accomplishments.

By paying attention to the thoughts that cross your mind and choosing which ones to listen to, you can regain your self-esteem and be comfortable with socializing.

Chapter 5. Mindful Strategies to Avoid Social Anxiety Relapse

Since you have reached this chapter, it is safe to assume that you are making progress in coping with your social anxiety. Now, you are ready to learn how to avoid mistakes and setbacks so that you will be able to overcome social anxiety relapse.

Before we proceed to the strategies though, you must first assess yourself as to whether you can handle it on your own. If you notice yourself exhibiting the following symptoms, it is best to seek a psychotherapist right away:

- You start to entertain thoughts of suicide.

Seek help from the national suicide hotline (1 800 SUICIDE) or from the emergency hotline. Do not hold yourself back because seeking help is the best thing you can do for yourself and your loved ones.

- You find it difficult to handle your depression and anxiety.

If you have lost interest in normal, everyday activities such as eating, working, and your hobbies, a professional can help you regain momentum in your life.

- None of the strategies seems to be working.

If, no matter how hard you tried, none of the strategies to overcome social anxiety has worked for you, then you may need professional guidance. It is possible that your doctor can identify other unnoticed factors.

- You are becoming addicted to certain substances.

Sometimes, it takes more than yourself to let go of alcoholism, drug addiction, or some other kind of substance abuse to cope with your anxiety. Find help from a trusted doctor, such as your family physician, to help keep you from falling into an addiction.

If you do not exhibit any of these signs and if you are confident that you can prevent a social anxiety relapse on your own, then here are the strategies to do so:

Be a Step Ahead of your Anxiety

During the days when you are feeling absolutely confident that you have overcome social anxiety, prepare for a contingency plan in case it creeps up on you. Not saying that it will, but if it does, it is wise to be prepared for it.

For instance, you can have a special affirmation to say to yourself in case you start to feel anxious. You can also be ready with a simple meditation technique that you can apply to help manage the symptoms.

Accept Your Anxiety when it happens

When your social anxiety does creep in, do not fight it,but at the same time do not react. Instead, acknowledge and accept it by saying,"I am feeling anxious right now and that is okay."Continue to be mindful of the present moment and then let it run its course.

Identify the Anxiety Trigger

In moments when you realize you are becoming increasingly anxious, it helps to remind yourself of your progress. It is also important to look into the mindfulness strategies and other techniques that were the most helpful to you in the past. That way, you can try applying them once again.

Gradually Increase your Exposure to Social Situations

Start small, but always keep moving forward so that you become more and more accustomed to being in a social situation. It is best to be exposed to a variety of social situations as well, but of course, you can do so gradually.

For instance, if you are highly anxious when you are

talking to strangers, start by having conversations with acquaintances, or people to whom you have already been introduced. Once you start to feel more comfortable, move on to talking to customer service people, who are trained to be friendly and helpful to you. After that, you can move on to talking to a neighbor, to introducing yourself to a new friend, to joining a club. You can progress through these steps in as short as a few months or as long as three years, it does not matter. What matters is you are slowly but surely learning to accept socializing.

Channel your Anxiety towards Something Healthy
The wonderful thing about mindfulness is it compels you to engage with what is going on in the present moment. That way, you would no longer be distracted by worrisome and fearful thoughts. If you notice that anxiety is starting to creep in, direct your focus towards a healthy and helpful activity, such as exercise, cooking a healthy meal, reading a good book, or listening to uplifting music. It will help you ride the waves of your emotions with ease.

Communicate with a Trusted Friend
If you have a friend you could trust, talk to that person regarding your social anxiety. I hope that he or she would also listen with compassion, understanding, and without criticism. Confide about your problems with dealing with social situations. He or she might even be able to help you out during certain situations in order to help you feel more comfortable.

Breathe out the Anxiety

A simple yet helpful technique to help you calm down when anxiety sets in is to breathe it out. Here are the steps:

Step 1: Become still and relaxed. You can sit or lie down, if you like, but you can also remain standing up.

Step 2: Breathe in deeply through your nose, and as you do, think of the words:"Confidence," "Happiness,"and"Strength."

Step 3: Hold your breath for a few seconds, visualizing these three words nourishing your mind and heart.

Step 4: Slowly breathe out through your lips. As you do, imagine your anxiety escaping through the breath and out of your body.

Continue to apply these steps until you feel completely filled with confidence, happiness, and strength.

Lastly, it is important to keep in mind that making mistakes does not mean all your hard work in the past is for nothing. There is no such thing as a perfectly paved way towards overcoming social anxiety, after all. What simply matters is you keep on going with a mindful attitude.

Conclusion

We all go through emotional highs and lows every day.
On some days, our emotions are relatively stable and
almost neutral. On others, we experience different ranges
of positive emotions, such as elation and pleasure, and
negative emotions, from disappointment to deep sorrow.
All the same, managing your emotions can be
challenging when they are intense, but the good news is
that mindfulness can help you do so.

As what you have already encountered in the previous
chapters, mindfulness strategies teach you how to pay
close attention–be fully aware of–your emotional,
mental, and physical state as well as the events that
surround you. It enables you to regulate yourself with a
sense of openness, compassion, and curiosity. It points
you back to the present moment, or the true reality that
you are in so that you would not be swept away by your
fears from the past or your worries about the future.

There is a multitude of mindfulness strategies you can
apply to regulate your emotional state in an instant. The
more frequently you practice mindfulness, the more
effortless it would be for you to manage even more
intense emotions. In this chapter, you will learn five of
the most effective mindfulness strategies to regain your
composure and stay grounded in the present moment in
the face of conflict.

If you try to imagine what deep relaxation feels like, it

would feel as if you are floating in the clouds, open, limitless, and carefree. You would be utterly immersed in the present moment, so much so that your mind is filled only with contentment, kindness, and gratitude. In today's fast-paced world, you might think that deep relaxation is unachievable, but the truth is that mindfulness meditation can help you get there.

Mindful Breathing Meditation
Mindful breathing meditation is the foundation of all formal mindfulness meditation exercises. Practicing it regularly will not only help you cope with anxiety, but also strengthen and lengthen your ability to concentrate on the present moment. It is important not to mistake mindful breathing for deep breathing. That is because in the former you are not advised to try to control your breathing, but rather to simply be aware of your natural breathing rhythm during that present moment.

The best thing about this mindfulness strategy is it can be done anywhere and at any time, whether you are sitting, standing, or even lying down. It can last for as short as five minutes to as much as an hour, if you so wish. However, if you are new to meditation you are advised to start small and then gradually work your way up.

Therefore, without further ado, here are the steps to practicing mindful breathing meditation:
Step 1: Begin by adopting a posture that combines dignity and comfort. Ensure that the back is straight and your shoulders are relaxed. If you wish, you may set your timer (doing so will prevent you from breaking out

of the meditative state just to check the time).

You can also light candles, play some relaxing instrumental background music, and adjust the room temperature, but only if you think this will help you improve your concentration.

Step 2: Allow your eyelids to relax. You do not have to close your eyes, but if it can help you concentrate, then do so. For a few minutes, allow your mind to become more open and curious towards the present moment. You can softly say,"I am here, now. I open my mind, my heart, and my senses to the present moment."

Step 3: Let your mind concentrate on your nostrils. Notice how your breath naturally moves into your nostrils, then travels down your windpipes, fills up your lungs, and expands your belly. Observe with nothing but pure curiosity how it starts to leave your lungs, causing your belly to deflate as it is pushed out through the windpipes and the nostrils once more. Continue to concentrate only on your natural breath until you hear the timer ring.

If your mind begins to wander towards thoughts unrelated to your breath, gently draw it back towards the feeling of your breath through your nostrils. Do not judge yourself for lingering in your thoughts though, as it is only natural for beginners to get distracted. Whenever a thought starts to plague your mind, think of the following words:"I am thinking, I am thinking…"to keep you anchored in the present moment. If the thought is something related to your anxiety, think,"I am worrying…I am worrying…"This way, you become an observer of your own thoughts, which will keep you from being consumed by them.

Mindfulness Meditation for Stress Relief
Psychologists define stress as a state of emotional or mental suspense or strain. It is triggered when the mind perceives something as dangerous, therefore stimulating the adrenal gland to release the steroid hormone cortisol. This hormone triggers a broad range of physical and mental symptoms, from chest pain, a rapid heart rate, and an upset stomach, to irritability, general unhappiness, and agitation.

One important consequence of stress is that it triggers the"flight or fight"response, enabling us to either escape from the source of danger or defend ourselves against it if we have to. While this proves itself useful in truly dangerous times, such as having to escape from a building on fire to fighting off a bully who is harming your kid brother, chronic stress will cause a lot of harm to your wellbeing. Unfortunately, those with social anxiety experience stress on a regular basis.

There are many ways to overcome chronic stress, from changing your diet, to exercising, to improving your sleeping habits, but the most basic of all is to change your outlook towards life. Keep in mind that stress begins in the mind, and if the mind perceives something as harmless as a telephone call as a threat, then it would always feel stressed.

The good news is that there is a mindfulness strategy to

help you significantly lower your stress levels when they set in. You can call it the stress-releasing mindfulness meditation. Here are the steps to apply it:

Step 1: Find a quiet, secure, and comfortable place where you can spend some time alone without anyone to disturb you. You may start the timer, if you wish.

Step 2: Sit or lie down with a comfortable yet confident posture. You may place your hands on your lap or knees if you are sitting, or you may rest them on top of your belly if you are lying down.

Step 3: Gently draw your full attention towards your breath. Notice the rhythm of your natural breath in the present moment. Are you breathing in an even, natural way, or holding your breath, or are you gasping?

Continue to be mindful of your breath without judgment or criticism.

Step 4: After a few minutes, gently move your focus towards the center of your chest. Become aware of the beating of your heart. Notice its pace in the present moment. Is it fast, or is it slow? Keep focusing on it for a few minutes with an open, compassionate, and curious attitude.

Step 5: After focusing on your heartbeat, calmly draw your attention up towards your mind. Become aware of the different thoughts, ideas, and emotions that are running through it. However, be a mere observer and do not engage with them. What are these thoughts in your mind? Which thoughts in particular are making you feel stressed? What kind of emotions are being stoked by these stressful thoughts?

Step 6: Allow your thoughts to run their course until they wear themselves out. Acknowledge and accept that you are now stressed out, but given enough time, your turbulent emotions and thoughts will subside.

Step 7: Gently draw your focus back towards your breath once your stressful thoughts begin to fade away. Continue to concentrate on your breath until you notice yourself start to breathe more evenly.

By becoming mindful of the physical and psychological symptoms of your stress, you will come to realize that it will not last forever. In other words, you will not get"caught up"in your stress but instead choose to let it run its course until it subsides. The more frequently you become mindful in times of stress, the sooner it is for you to recover from its symptoms. With a clear and calm mind, you can then approach whatever issue you have at present in a healthy way.

The Body Scan Meditation
The Body Scan meditation is a highly effective mindfulness strategy when it comes to reducing not only emotional but also physical stress. Primarily, it helps you become more in tune with your body, which draws your focus away from all your ideas, judgments, beliefs, desires, worries, and other such thoughts. Listening to your own body will help you understand yourself from a different perspective.

To do the Body Scan Meditation, it is best to set aside at least 30 minutes of your time, which is well worth it. If you do not feel comfortable with this length, perhaps it is best for you to try doing the body scan with your upper body only in one session, and then with your lower body in the next session.

Here are the steps to doing the Body Scan Meditation: Step 1: Find a nice, quiet place where you can lie down and not be disturbed for a while. You can lie down on a mat on the floor, on a couch that is large enough to accommodate your entire body, or on your bed.

Step 2: Next, loosen any tightness in your clothing, jewelry, and so on, particularly around the armpits, neck, waist, and thighs. Ideally, you are to take off your shoes (but you can keep your socks on). You may set a timer, if you wish.

Step 3: Lie down and gently rest your arms by your sides with your palms facing the ceiling or sky. Let your legs be comfortably and naturally apart. You may place a cushion beneath your knees or neck if it makes you feel more comfortable. You can even cover yourself with a blanket.

If lying down is not possible for you, simply sit up in a comfortable and relaxed way.

Step 4: When you are ready, begin by concentrating on how it feels to be lying down. Notice how your weight is pressed against that mat or bed, particularly in the areas of your body that are touching it.

Step 5: Transition your focus towards your natural breath. Notice how your breath enters and leaves your body and how it causes your belly to inflate and deflate with each inhale and exhale. Maintain this concentration for as long as you like.

Step 6: Shift your focus towards the sensations in your right foot. With curiosity and openness, become aware of the kind of sensations it feels. Does your right foot feel cold or warm? If you are wearing socks, how does the fabric feel against your foot? What are the sensations in between the toes? On the other hand, is there no sensation in your right foot? Even the lack of feeling can also be noticed.

Step 7: Breathe in naturally and as you do, visualize the breath flowing into your right foot. As you breathe out, imagine it flowing back up out or your nose. Continue to"breathe into and out of"your right foot.

Step 8: Expand your focus towards your entire right leg. Notice the sensations felt by your ankle, calf, knee, and thigh. Breathe into and out of your entire right leg.

Step 9: Repeat the same steps with your left foot and then leg. All the while, continue to nourish feelings of curiosity, compassion, and openness towards these body parts.

Step 10: Transition your focus towards the area around your pelvis, buttocks, and hips. Notice any sensations–or lack thereof–in these areas. Then, breathe into them as well.

Step 11: Allow your mind's observant eye to travel up to your lower abdominal area and back. Begin by focusing on the movements of your belly as the air enters and leaves your lungs. Notice any sensations felt in this part of your core without judgment.

Step 12: Draw your attention towards the upper torso, where you have your upper back, chest, and shoulders. Notice how your breath causes your rib cage to expand and then contract with each in-and out-breath.

Listen to the beating of your heart and feel a sense of openness and compassion towards it. Appreciate your lungs for ceaselessly functioning to maintain your entire body. Notice the emotions that are evoked during this moment, and then observe them for a while.

Step 13: Shift your focus gently towards the tips of your fingers. Become aware of the sensations in them. Breathe into and out of your fingers for several minutes, visualizing the oxygen nourishing their delicate and sensitive parts.

Step 14: Gradually expand your focus towards your hands, then your arms, and shoulders. Continue to notice any sensations felt in each of these parts, taking your time to acknowledge and accept each of them as you go. Then, breathe into your arms, allowing the oxygen to carry nourishment through them.

Step 15: Concentrate on your neck area. Be fully aware of the sensations felt around and in it as you continue to breathe naturally. Draw your focus up towards your jaw and notice the muscles, if there is any tension. Breathe into and out of the muscle fibers within your neck and jaw.

Step 16: Shift your focus towards your face area, particularly your eyes, nose, and cheeks. Become aware of the sensations felt in each area and notice if there is any tension in it. Take care not to attempt to correct anything unless it feels natural to you.

Step 17: Gradually draw your attention towards the back of your head and then to the top of your head, scanning for any sensations felt, or acknowledging the absence of sensations. Breathe into and out of your entire head, visualizing the energy from each breath filling and nurturing all the cells inside and around your skull. Continue to do this for several minutes.

Step 18: When you are ready, begin a whole-body scan starting with the top of your head down to the tips of your toes. Notice all the sensations and emotions felt across your entire body. Continue to breathe into every fiber of your being. Stay in this meditative state for as long as you like, or until you hear the gentle ring of your timer.

After practicing this mindfulness strategy, you will notice that it helps you let go of any tense emotions kept deep inside. Often, these emotions are buried so deep they would manifest into some sort of physical discomfort, such as indigestion, headaches, or back pain. By practicing body scan meditation regularly, your pent up emotions will be released and hopefully, so will your aches and pains.

Mindfully Facing Anxious Emotions

Sometimes, establishing the right attitude towards your anxiety is the first step towards changing it. This attitude is one in which you do not fear the anxiety as it sets in, but rather let the anxiety be there as you calmly watch it rise and then fall. As a result, you would no longer struggle with the emotion.

To apply this strategy, follow these steps:
Step 1: Notice how you would usually react to anxiety as soon as it sets in. Observe the current attitude you have towards it.

Step 2: Think about the kind of impact of a mindful attitude would have on your feelings of anxiety. Adopt a calm, observant, and open mind as you notice the anxiety build up for a few minutes.

Step 3: Breathe into the area in your body and mind where the anxiety manifests itself the most strongly. Do this for a few minutes.

Step 4: In your mind's eye, become aware of the anxiety taking shape. Does the emotion have a color, texture, and a shape? Which part of the body do you feel the anxiety most strongly? How intense is it on a scale of one to ten? Continue to explore the anxiety like a visitor would a painting at a museum.

Step 5: Acknowledge that you have the anxiety, and accept the fact that you can feel it. Then, watch it fade away.

Lastly, I want you to be yourself, you are unique human being so stop worrying what others think of you, worry about what you think of yourself, nothing matters more.

ABOUT THE AUTHOR

Mike Bray, an avid admirer of human body, spirit and mental health and a careful observer of its multiple functions, a person who has hands on training experience and is devoted to sharing all this knowledge he has acquired with all of you, is your guide that will explicitly walk you through the process of controlling your emotions while feeling anxius.

Mike interviewed many doctors throughout writing this book, just to ensure his informations are right and supported by experiences and facts.

Getting all of these informations was not easy, but Mike himself is convinced that it was worth it , because he could get all of this informations into ONE single book, covering all the important points of social anxiety.

Call for Review
Thank you very much for buying my book, hopefully you get the value you want to get. Please, if you found this book helpful, review it on amazon pages so that other people can see pros and cons of this book, and as well it is very good indicator for me as an author what to improve, avoid or keep. Thank you very much!

www.ingramcontent.com/pod-product-compliance
Lightning Source LLC
Chambersburg PA
CBHW050456290526
45786CB00006B/2310